A Rocket Boy Grows Up

Homer looked up at the October sky. He could see millions of stars. He could see a few planets.

"Look, look!" his friend O'Dell said, pointing up in the sky.

"I see it, too," said Roy Lee.

Then Homer saw it! His eyes followed a bright light streaking across the night sky.

It was 1957. Homer Hickam had just seen *Sputnik*. It was an amazing sight!

Sputnik was the first space satellite. Russia launched *Sputnik* on October 5, 1957. The name "Sputnik" comes from Russian where it means "satellite" or "fellow traveler."

Russia and the United States were in a "race to space." People in the U.S. had hoped that America would be the first into space. After *Sputnik*, the U.S. worked hard on the space race.

Sputnik

Homer Hickam Jr. was one of the many American kids who dreamed of flying rockets. He wanted to be a rocket scientist. And you know what? His dream came true. But it wasn't easy making that dream come true.

Homer lived in Coalwood, West Virginia. His father was the coal mine foreman. Almost everyone in town worked for the underground mine. It was hard work and not much money. No one in Coalwood had much money, but they encouraged their children to do well in school.

Homer was 14 years old in 1957. He went to Big Creek High School. His school bus had to travel over two mountains to get to the school. He loved science class. His science teacher, Miss Freida Riley, wanted all her students to work hard and do their best in school.

Miss Freida Riley

Homer knew a lot about science, but he didn't know that much about rockets in 1957. He asked a boy named Quentin for help. Quentin already knew a lot about rockets. He spent weekends at the library reading everything he could.

Soon the two boys were talking rockets and drawing plans nonstop. O'Dell, Sherman, Roy Lee, and Billy joined them.

The boys called themselves the "Rocket Boys of the Big Creek Missile Agency." Other people started calling them the Rocket Boys, too.

Homer mixed and tested the rocket fuel. The boys shot off the first rocket in Homer's backyard. It was not a success and burnt part of the fence.

Homer was part of a Rocketry Club like this.

Homer Hickam, Quentin Wilson, Roy Lee Cooke, and Jimmy O'Dell Carroll

The Rocket Boys started building other rockets. Some went far. Some just fizzled. They kept trying.

They launched rockets in big open areas. They measured how high and how far each rocket went. Their rockets were getting better and better. They were flying higher and farther.

People in Coalwood were catching rocket fever. People would drive out to watch Homer and his friends launch their rockets.

Some people offered to help. Mr. Ferro at the machine shop told Homer to draw a picture of the parts he needed. Mr. Ferro helped make special round parts of steel.

A lot of people believed the Rocket Boys would really take off.

One of Homer's heroes was a rocket scientist named Wernher von Braun. Dr. von Braun directed the United States space program. He helped the United States become a leader in the "race to space."

One day a large brown envelope came for Homer. Inside was an autographed picture of Dr. von Braun and a personal note to Homer. It said: "If you work hard enough, you will do anything you want."

Homer kept studying hard and working hard. He believed what Dr. von Braun had written in his note.

One day, Miss Riley asked Homer to enter a science fair.

Dr. Wernher von Braun

Homer and his friends entered the county science fair. They made a display to show the science behind rockets. They made posters with drawings of their rockets and the direction they flew. One poster showed lots of numbers. It takes a lot of math to be able to figure out how to make a rocket fly!

They won! Their rocket display won first place at the McDowell County Science Fair.

Homer went on to the National Science Fair in Indianapolis, Indiana. No one from Coalwood, West Virginia, had ever made it to something like the National Science Fair.

But something terrible happened at the science fair. Someone stole part of Homer's display, including some rocket parts. Now there was no chance of winning.

Homer with his science project

National Science Fair

A STUDY OF AMATEUR ROCKETRY TECHNIQUES

Homer H. Hickam, Jr.

Big Creek High School

War, West Virginia

Gold and Silver
Medal Award
1960

Sponsored by: Pocahontas Industrial Council for Education
Bluefield State College

The National Science Fair is a Science Clubs of America – Science Service
activity conducted in cooperation with leading newspapers,
educational, industrial and civic organizations

TAKES FIRST PLACE—*A Study of Rocketry Techniques won a first place in the*
960 McDowell County Science Fair for Homer (Sonny) Hickam, Big Creek High
chool Senior. Homer's physics teacher is Miss Frieda Riley and his parents are Mr. and
rs. Homer Hickam of Coalwood. (Daily News Photo by The Wa......

14

Homer called his mother. It was the first time he'd ever made a long distance phone call. Mrs. Hickam got help from the people in Coalwood. Homer's father had never helped before. But this time he did! Homer knew that his father was proud of him and his rockets.

New rocket parts arrived for Homer at eight o'clock the next morning. Homer rushed the parts back to the science fair.

No one really thought six poor boys from a coal-mining town could win. But Homer and his friends proved that they could do anything they wanted to do. They won first place in the nation!

The people in Coalwood were proud of their Rocket Boys. All the boys worked hard to earn money so they could go to college. Winning their gold medal showed them that they could do anything.

Homer wrote a book about his life called *Rocket Boys*. The book was made into a movie called *October Sky*. If you take all the letters from "rocket boys" and scramble them, you can get the words "October sky."